The Upside Down Circle

What is Zen? Zen is a realization of Absolute Reality . . . which is life, the Source. You are Zen, but not the personal you as provided by ordinary mind.

Many books available today translate centuries-old verbal exchanges between monks and Zen Masters. These stories depict monks asking questions that seem simple and understandable. Yet the answers they received from the Masters were often irrelevant, illogical, and confusing.

To break habitual thinking patterns, Zen Masters often give their students a koan, a question which cannot be answered logically. This twist in normal thinking often becomes a catalyst for the person to enter into a new relationship with his or her own thinking process. One then experiences the immediacy of the present moment—the flow of life—without resistance.

Since this world is constantly changing—and we realize nothing is permanent—the fluid teachings of Zen are eminently adaptable to our Western world, as Zen Master Gilbert illustrates so artfully in these "teaching cartoons."

His main character, Unk, seeks truth and happiness. But time and again, he merely bumbles his way from one confusion to another, mistaking the moon in the water as reality. With the help of his friend, Pepito, and his teacher, Master Woof, Unk eventually learns that when ordinary little mind is free to see clearly, the real moon has merely been hidden by clouds of concepts. Only when he climbs the mountain and views the whole panorama, can he truly laugh at all the little clouds of worldly entanglement and glimpse, perhaps for the first time, the exquisite beauty and natural freedom of all life.

The Upside Down Circle

Publishing by Blue Dolphin Publishing, Inc.
P.O. Box 8, Nevada City, CA 95959
Orders: 1-800-643-0765
Web: www.bluedolphinpublishing.com

ISBN: 0-931892-18-X

Library of Congress Cataloging-in-Publication Data

Gilbert, Don.
    The upside down circle.

    1. Zen Buddhism—Caricatures and cartoons.   I. Title.
BQ9265.6.G55 1988   294.3'4   88-7455
ISBN 0-931892-18-X

Printed in the United States of America

9   8   7   6   5   4   3   2

This book is dedicated to Dawn Bill
to thank her for her constant effort
in helping in the production of this book.

Today, as we become more interested in modern approaches to developing creativity and intuition, it is rewarding to find a book inspired by the richness of the ancient Zen meditation tradition that speaks so directly the these interests.

With a gentle smile and sometimes with a hearty laugh, Zen Master Gilbert points beyond the confines of our habitual views and established institutions. His unique style of teaching is an integration of original artwork, commentary and humor that is at once light-hearted and enjoyable.

Just beneath this innocent-looking surface, though, **The Upside Down Circle** contains teachings of the profoundest order. Perhaps this book will lead you, too, with a laugh or a gasp, to knowings and feelings that open in time like flowers in gardens somehow outside the limitations of conditioned awareness.

—Will Tuttle, Ph.D.

CONTENTS

INTRODUCTION

WHAT IS ZEN? Zen is a realization of Absolute Reality. It is life, the Source. You are Zen, but not the *personal* you as provided by ordinary mind.

Historically, Zen Buddhism was said to have been brought by a monk named Bodhidharma from India to China around 570 A.D. It originated in Mahayana Buddhism and was originally known in China as Ch'an. Later, Ch'an spread to Korea where it was known as Sön. Finally, it spread to Japan where it became known as Zen.

Though Zen, Ch'an, and Sön do not have teachings that are exclusive or different from the traditional Buddhist schools before Bodhidharma, there is a major difference in the way of their practices. These schools are and were, to say the least, unusual. Their practices are full of puzzling statements, confusing attitudes, and teaching methods that can be shockingly surprising.

After the ninth century, various schools slowly incorporated the practices into the arts and into many of the ordinary activities of life. The teachings and practices penetrated the areas of painting, poetry, calligraphy, flower arranging, the tea ceremony, the martial arts and archery, to name a few.

Many books are available today which translate centuries-old mondos (verbal exchanges) between monks and Zen Masters. These stories depict monks asking Zen questions that seem simple and understandable. Yet, the answers they received from the Zen Masters were often irrelevant, illogical, and confusing. Consider that the masters may have tried to get the questioners to drop their 'habit thinking,' the mind's logical problem-solving approach, in order to help the monks awaken to an area beyond the confines of the simple intellect. To fully sense the meaning of a master's response required a direct, intuitive experience.

To break this chain of logic, Zen Masters often gave their students a *koan*, a question which could not be answered logically and yet required an 'answer.' For instance, one of the ancient and honored koans is the question, "What is the meaning of Bodhidharma's coming from the West?" Master Tung Shan's reply was, "I will tell you when the mountain stream flows back." This reply truly places the answer right under one's nose.

Why does Zen seem so ungraspable? Perhaps because it has no philosophies to teach, and it appears to be full of contradictions. Zen does not try to teach methods to avoid or deny the world: it is not a method of resisting the motion of life. Rather, it is a way to know life and to move with it—to act according to the changes and courses that life is fulfilling.

Zen is a way of courage and faith: courage to face and be what one is in the fullest sense, and faith that a greater *knowing* can be present if one will stop trying to arrest the motion of the world.

The world is a world of change, and the changing is its perfection. We cannot grasp perfection and hold onto it (as Unk tries to do in this book). For no 'thing' could be absolutely perfect. If it were, it would be dead, changeless. Yet, even death is a form of change as the thing involved decays. This decay can be seen as a way to reassemble the materials involved to create newer forms.

If one decides to undertake Zen practice, it is well to remember that the practice is not a small hill one must climb, but a formidable mountain. Reading books can be useful, but the implementation of the practice is of primary importance. One does not need a lot of cookbooks if one doesn't intend to spend time in the kitchen. Though Zen may provide one with a raft and an oar, one must 'shoot the rapids' on one's own.

Since people vary in disposition, ability, and state of knowing, the Zen Master must provide instructions that fit the situation. It should be remembered that as the teaching moved into various countries throughout the centuries, the methods of practice were modified by the cultural structure in the host country. The cultural adaptations were needed to provide an acceptable entry into the effort.

Today, Zen forms (i.e., Zen teachings and methods) must be refined to the demands of the twentieth century if Zen is to stay alive in the West. Therefore, to present a 'Western' Zen requires an understanding of the world view that is current in the West. 'Western' Zen should not be an effort to impose other cultural standards upon itself but should communicate in a manner familiar to its listeners.

And yet, it must be recognized that Zen is beyond the cultural limitations that may be present in the manner of its presentation. For true intuitive knowing cannot be restricted by any patterns imposed by cultures, religions, politics, or selfish aims. The basic Truth will underlie all manners of approach, yet the idea of a manner of approach must be transcended. So, even to declare oneself a 'Zenist' is to deny Zen.

Therefore, the approach to Truth is not the issue: mankind itself is the problem with its limited view of Reality. Inner growth, inner expansion is needed.

Perhaps there should first be a close look at how the mind works. Maybe this can show us how suspect are the concepts and convictions of ordinary mind. For things that are developed in and by intelligence will reflect all of the shortcomings inherent in the capricious, ordinary (logical) mind. The use of intelligence is often guided by misunderstandings, faulty convictions, fear, greed, ill will, and an effort to make others conform to certain ideas. When the logical mind can see how illogical it truly is, then perhaps the way can be open to intuitional knowing.

Humor is a key to knowing because it depends on intuitive flashes that reveal the Truth and the incongruities in the subject at hand. Humor is a romp: it is open and fun-filled. It is in this attitude of openness that one can participate and have flashes of insight.

Unk in this book is portrayed as a bumbler. But, he hangs in there. He illustrates many of the errors that show up in practice. Yet, he truly wants to know. Within Unk's struggles are humorous situations that are in a sense "fingers pointing at the moon" of enlightenment—the moon that is always there but hidden by the clouds of concept.

In the story, Unk is constantly being hit by the Zen Master's stick. When Unk gets to sailing off in his intellectual misdirections, the Zen Master halts these activities with an abrupt, irreversible stinging moment in the Now. He is constantly providing Unk with the answer to the aforementioned koan that should sooner or later bring Unk to a knowing when "the mountain stream flows back."

When we climb the mountain and rise above the clouds, the beauty of Truth is revealed. Henceforth, we can laugh at the clouds of the world. Yet, they too have a beauty and reality previously unrecognized.

THE QUEST

UNK IS ABOUT TO EXPERIENCE what to him is a search for enlightenment. He views this experience as a self-initiated quest, and he feels that if he is successful, he will become a true knower—a sage.

This very attitude is rooted in the notion maintained in the logical mind that all problems must be solved by the intellect. Behind this notion lies the effort to objectify everything, including oneself, and to carefully assemble these objectified bits into a whole and complete truth. However, the objective world is merely a mind creation.

Logical mind is very illogical about its own constitution. It sees itself as an object, a conceptualization of itself as provided by the bits and pieces of its own conceptualizing. Thus, the one called 'Unk' is an illusion living the illusion of an objective reality. He is the 'great pretender,' the self-notion that feels that he can modify this life-dream according to his own designs. All this is part of the fantasy.

Therefore, Unk has to awaken from the notion of being Unk. The truth of Unk is not 'thingly.' There is nothing to be found (no thingly thing) nor anyone to find it. The unfindable is what Unk is, and this unfindable is the found. So no matter how assiduously Unk looks within, he can never see the seer.

The truth is that Unk wants to live for his own pleasures and gain. His seeking only strengthens his conviction that he is a distinct and separate being moving toward goals objectified in his mind as being 'out there.' Yet, the burden and the binding that are constantly present when this objectified pseudo-self predominates can never produce freedom. So, for Unk to seek Zen through conceptualization is an exercise in futility. It is merely another form of objectification.

Many of us have been entertained by the antics of the 'Muppets' as they appeared on television. If Unk could realize that he is being *lived*, as are these little figures, then perhaps he would stop trying to write the script for this great appearance, and his True Nature would stand unimpeded.

The goal is not a goal, nor is it not 'not a goal.' *Knowing* is the key, and all logical or conceptual efforts are ego manifestations.

The unattainable must be attained; the unknowable, known. But not by *you* or *me*.

Effort must be effortless, a simple fulfilling of that which is. Not a description—just a fulfilling.

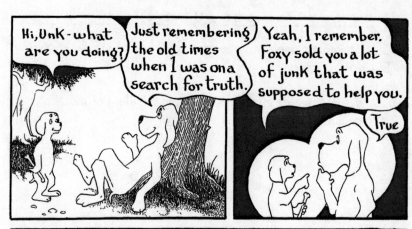

•

Long ago Unk was an avid seeker of Truth. In the book, *Jellyfish Bones*, his search was hard and fruitless, so Unk gave up. Now he hungers again for an answer. He may be in for a surprise if he expects Master Woof to provide it.

5

·

In simple terms, enlightenment indicates the absence of the illusion of self and other.

The 'YOU' Master Woof speaks of is an object. This of course implies a subject. Subject and object is the illusion that obscures enlightenment.

Hence, Master Woof's statement points that wherever 'YOU' go, enlightenment will be hidden. He indicates that there must be a wholeness, not the persistence of a dichotomy.

8

•

Zen is something that must be realized, it cannot be taught. If one merely believes in Zen, one has missed it.

The stick is direct and meaningful and brings attention to life right where it is. These whacks with the stick are really keys that can provide an opening to the very source of life (Zen).

10

•

It sounds as if Unk is saying that 'nowhere' is somewhere. How could this 'nowhere' really be nowhere? If Unk is nowhere, he would then be somewhere.

●

There are many philosophies, yet the confusion continues. For explanations may be clever and convincing and still be lacking wisdom.

Unk misses the point. He thinks of himself as an objective entity. His last statement shows how completely he is functioning in an attitude of duality.

This 'me' that Unk thinks of as himself is part of the collection of ideas and concepts that fill his ordinary mind. This is a pseudo-self. However, the True Self, the *observing awareness* that makes consciousness possible, is not an object. Yet all objects appear within it.

Ikkyu, a great Japanese Zen Master (1394-1481), wrote the following verse that points directly at the pseudo-self,

"The mind of man is without sound, without odor; he who answers when called is nothing but a thief."

•

Unk (so-called) is assuming that there is a questioner and answerer. He also assumes that Zen is a thing. The term 'Zen' indicates the force that causes all the images in life to appear.

If Unk seeks Unk, no thing will be found. Can the seeker find the seeker? Can an eye see itself?

To find the Real, mind must escape the imprisoning circle of conditioning it has built.

•

Strange. The immediacy of life is ever present but seldom recognized for what it is.

Now is what we are. It cannot be a goal or state to attain. *Now* is the activity of the moment before the thoughts mislabel it.

18

•

_____

Here, Unk has been given a koan. The Zen
koan poses a question or makes a statement that
is not logical. Though the koan does not make
sense in the customary fashion, one must give
the Zen Master an 'answer.' Try as it may, the
logical mind can find no answer. The struggle
goes on and on until (perhaps) the intellect
freezes in its tracks, providing the intuitive
aspect of mind a moment of quiet opportunity.
Now a fuller knowing is present without the
hampering limitations of the objectifying mind
warping the results.

_____

Master Woof, meet Doctor Bright. The doctor is a scientist.

He says this circle was produced by the best scientific equipment.

Best brains also!

So?

He says, too, that since it is a perfect circle, it cannot be upside down.

Impossible!

A simple test, Doctor. Are you over there?

How simple can you get? Sure I'm over here.

Tell me where the circle is.

It's right there by you.

There's your proof, Doc—your circle is upside down.

•

Western minds generally have a predilection for seeking the infinite with finite methods. This logical approach is one of dissection and assembling. The pieces are arranged (in mind) in seemingly sensible sequences in order to provide an answer. The problem is that even the most brilliant minds have a distinct and limited supply of 'mind material' from which to draw.

Doctor Bright is a perfect example of logic seeking the infinite. He thinks perfection can be devised by rational, scientific methods. In addition, he sees himself as being apart from the circle, the appearances (subject/object) arising in the conditioned mind.

Can the circle truly be seen when it is being judged by a logical (incomplete) mind?

•

Foxy represents the exploiters—those who prey on people who are earnestly seeking the Truth.

Unk has had many dealings with Foxy in the past, but he still deals with him whenever he is offered a seemingly easy solution to his problem. He listens to Woof, but he buys from Foxy.

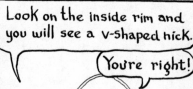

●

Will Unk buy this explanation? After all, he did buy the hula hoop.

•

The hula hoop is not the Upside Down Circle. The logical mind can measure, but not perfectly. If you live in the center of your concepts and convictions that surround you, how can you know this circle is perfect? You are whatever distortions your mind-circle is, and it never really hangs perfectly in every direction.

28

·

Unk seeks to rise above worldly things. He seeks a spiritual world and he thinks he must deny worldly activities. Master Woof is pointing out that he cannot separate the spiritual from the worldly. Unk should fulfill his worldly and spiritual activities in normal daily living.

•

In general Buddhist terms, *dharma* is used to refer to the teachings of the Buddha. In another sense, it refers to the social law or the fulfilling of one's personal duty according to one's nature and innate abilities.

In the Zen teachings, *Dharma* means Self Nature. Self Nature cannot be seen or discerned by the thinking mind. It is void. The Self Nature of man is not of the body or mind, or of the things known by them. It is the *source* of the appearances of all things—including body and mind.

The direct experiences that Unk has in this sequence of events are openings to the Truth. If there was a full, experiential knowing of the infinite Source, or Dharma, his search would be over.

32

•

Though the world appears divided, it is the One—which is indeterminate and undifferentiated. But human consciousness cannot function in a condition of 'one-ness.' It requires a duality in order to be present.

Mind, or the Absolute, should neither be considered as 'one' nor any other number. The message is that consciousness functions in duality while supported by the one-ness.

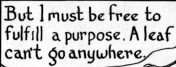

34

•

Mankind is generally looking for a purpose in life. This purpose is generally of a selfish or egotistic nature. In addition, the search for purpose implies that there is individual freedom of choice.

Freedom of choice, however, is truly non-freedom because the choices are dependent on the movement in logical mind. Thus, one is limited to one's conditioning.

•

Woof is saying that the secret of life is
revealed when we are living in harmony with the
changes and motions of life—when we are not
constantly struggling to change what is.

38

•

When the phenomenal world is seen as the only reality, one is held by the bondage of ignorance.

To feel that one is enlightened and has transcended the phenomenal world is equally a bondage of ignorance.

40

$$0 \times 0 + 0 \div 0 = 0$$

MEDITATION

MEDITATION IS A KEYSTONE in the search for the Self Nature. The obfuscations inherent in our minds require that the meditation practice first attend to the constant conflict between our emotions and our intellect. By some method, one must bring about a complete and unchangeable harmony between the two.

The beginning meditative practices thus focus on taming the ceaseless thought processes in the mind. The intent, however, is not to create a blank, thoughtless mind. Rather, through meditation one begins to attend to the things at hand with full attention.

43

The teachings say that if the breath can be tamed, one's mind will be tamed. Therefore, there is a simple practice that is almost universally used in Buddhist schools for beginning students. This practice is the 'counting of the breath.'

To begin, one may sit in any one of a variety of postures (full-lotus, half-lotus, kneeling, or seated in a chair). The back should be straight and the head erect. Breathe naturally and count either the inhalation or exhalation. Count from one to ten, and then start over. Continue for thirty minutes. Each breath and count should receive full attention. One sitting period in the morning and one in the evening are recommended, even if they are for shorter periods.

Though this practice may seem simple, the mind often wanders, and it is difficult to count to ten with full attention. However, if one truly wants to apply oneself to the practice, this constant effort must be made.

When one has achieved a certain mastery of the breathing practice, there are other traditional meditation practices available. They are practices that use mantras, chants, physical activities, koans, or Serene Reflection. These are all excellent and useful.

The koan practice is a mind exercise that is in its very method of declaration completely illogical. This illogical question or statement requires an intuitive response. Perhaps it is better to say that if the koan is successful, then awakening occurs. An example of a classic Zen koan is, "What is the sound of one hand clapping?"

Koan practice requires constant attention and effort. It is by nature a tension practice. Many of us living in a society filled with constant changes, problems, and distractions find our lives already subject to strong, ongoing tension. For some of us, then, other practices may be more suitable.

Serene Reflection (or Zazen Only) is a practice quite different from koan practice. The mind is quieted and does not respond to arising thoughts and words. 'Serene' implies more than just calmness or quietude, and 'reflection' does not mean to contemplate on some subject. Rather, there is clear and mirror-like awareness. It is bright, illuminating, and pure.

In either the koan or Serene Reflection practice, the design is to create mind conditions that open the way to intuitive knowing. The aim is satori, the 'seeing of Reality.' With satori, there is a comprehensive view of Reality, and it is now that one can commence true practice.

46

•

As long as Unk persists in searching for his True Self 'out there,' the truth remains hidden. As long as there is a conscious intention of attaining something, an obstacle is in the way of awakening.

•

Even though sitting in meditation is very helpful, it has limited uses. If there is a breakthrough to the highest intuitive level, then every motion of life is a meditation.

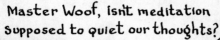

Master Woof, isn't meditation supposed to quiet our thoughts?

Yes

Well, when I sit and count my breath, each count is a thought.

When I repeat a mantra, thoughts are involved.

When I work on a koan, thought is present. How do I stop thinking?

Think of the unthinkable!

What's up Unk? I'm trying to think of an unthinkable think but an unthinkable think is unthinkable.

Unk is stumped

Yeah He was up a tree.

50

•

This points to Serene Reflection, the aware state of mind where the thoughts that arise are not pursued. Krishnamurti, a renowned teacher of the twentieth century, referred to Serene Reflection as 'choiceless awareness.'

To illustrate, visualize that one is seated in a dense forest at night. Imagine that it is totally dark—no moon, no stars, not a breath of air stirring. Also imagine that you know there is a tiger somewhere nearby. Would you not be listening intently?

The practice is one of utter receptivity, just as you would have if you were listening for the faintest sound that would signal the tiger's presence. There is no listener or thing listened to. Just pure listening.

Mind is like a mirror—pure reflection with no retention.

•

Some of us feel that if we adopt the clothes and manners of the culture from which our meditation originates, that we are now somehow truly on the path. There is danger here that we will thus adopt externals for the Truth.

·

With every self-affirmation of humility, the ego expands in scope and power.

True humbleness is unaware of humility.

Meditation is neither self-important nor self-denying.

•

Merely imitating even the most respected and accomplished teacher is missing the basic truth of this great inner effort. Your mountain is not the teacher's mountain. The student should continue with sincere, constant attention to his or her own practice.

•

This story is taken from a very famous koan given by Joshu, a great Zen Master (778-897). A monk asked Joshu, "Does a dog have Buddha Nature?" Joshu answered, "Mu" (No).

On the surface, this is contrary to Buddhist teachings which state that all creeping things with life have the Buddha Nature (Self Nature). However, if we reflect on the deeper translation of 'Mu' as 'no thing—not no thing,' we can see the depth of this reply.

•
___

Have you ever taken the time to examine your own junkyard (your conditioning, concepts, prejudices, and beliefs)?
___

61

•

Master Woof is pointing to a basic premise of Zen. With the attitude of 'I hear—I see—I speak,' there persists the belief in a judge who places values on things and events.

This judge seemingly makes choices in what decisions should be made and what actions should be taken. If the entity's actions are in keeping with the ideas present in mind, the entity feels it initiated a successful action. If the unfoldment of the moment is contrary to the impulses that were in mind, frustration ensues and there is a seeming failure.

However, this judge is not the determinant. If the law of cause and effect is true, then this moment in time already determines the next moment. Perhaps there is no cause and effect, but a consciousness of continuity that is only visible in universal quantum flashes.

When there is only hearing, seeing, and speaking, this is the 'action of non-action.' This action is direct and intuitional. It is the fulfillment of each moment without the interference of the judge. Life becomes a constant meditation. Standing, sitting, or lying down, one is living in the Now, and the way is smooth even though the way of the world is hilly.

•

Are we really meditating, or are we trying to escape the world? For some of us, meditation can be like hiding in a barrel.

Perhaps the Truth hides there with us.

66

•

Unk is simply traveling from one dream state to another.

MIND

MIND REFERS TO THAT WHICH IS beyond definition. This Mind is not just thoughts and thinking processes as experienced in everyday consciousness. It is *pure consciousness*.

When one attempts to 'look within' to find Truth, one generally only succeeds in seeing all the samsaric (worldly) limitations and imperfections as reflected by the logical mind and its limitations and imperfections. This mind is like a hall of funny mirrors in which the reflections are distorted according to the distortions in the mirrors.

Zen is concerned with direct *knowing* of Mind, not philosophies or woven thinking patterns. For example, when one is in a garden filled with beautiful yellow roses, the seeing is yellow. This is a knowing, not a matter of thought.

Mind is always present. Like sunshine, it provides life. We cannot produce it, and yet we always know it. When ordinary mind is 'set aside,' there is a realization of 'at-onement' with Mind. This is referred to as samādhi. The ordinary mind then resides in a natural condition of absolute tranquillity. The functions of ordinary mind continue, but the source of activity is not based on learned, conceptual ideas. It is a mode of intuitive knowing.

Conceptually, ordinary mind and Mind seem to be opposites. Yet, they are not truly divided—only in appearance.

To illustrate, imagine that there is a very large box sitting in the sun. There are a number of holes in the top of the box. If you had an inside view of the box, you would see little shafts of light coming through each one of the holes. Let us also imagine that each little light shaft is conscious. The rays look at each other, each feeling that it has its own consciousness separate from the consciousnesses of the other rays.

Now, suppose that the consciousness of one of the rays rises up the shaft and out through the hole in the box into the full sunlight. It realizes then that all the rays are in truth the one source (the sun). Upon reentering the hole into the box, that ray no longer has the sense of separation still present in the other rays. It could not, however, communicate this knowing to the other rays. At best, it could only encourage other rays to peek out through the hole to discover their wholeness.

70

•

It is apparent that Unk seeks a reasonable explanation to most of the Zen Master's attempts to point beyond the world of objectivity. For Unk, there is no singularity unless it can be explained dualistically.

•

Each motion of life is transmitted by the sensory system to a center of cognition that receives the input. This creates a feeling of a 'me' that constantly grows and is reinforced by every activity. Soon it becomes so firmly entrenched that awakening is very difficult.

Woof is trying here to shatter the process of this image-making.

74

•

The conditioned mind can only ask a conditioned question. Answers reflect the conditioning of the answerer. The answerer's answers are heard according to the conditioning of the mind hearing the answer.

•

Each pup thinks he knows in which way he wants to go.

Climbing the mountain, one finds the view unobstructed at the top. This is intuitional knowing. All directions are now 'one direction.'

The 'one direction' springs forth from pure consciousness or Mind.

78

•

A monk once asked a Zen Master, "Can you show me what Mind is?"

"Right there! Right there!" said the Master pointing to a pile of manure.

80

•

Unk is a habit machine. He's in the habit of creating a collection of more habits.

The more that this collection grows, the more firmly the conviction that these concepts have a true objective reality.

82

•

The teachings refer to 'dust' as the collection of concepts in mind and our persistent clinging to them. Pure consciousness remains hidden by this dust, and the True Self is obscured by the pseudo-self created by the dust itself.

84

•

One of the biggest problems of so-called 'practices' is that the practice itself becomes a habit. The belief sets in that there is a practicer, someone who is on his way—a traveler who is going where he is already.

•

Can one rinse out the muddy mind? Can a habit pattern overcome a habit pattern without creating another habit pattern?

How can a collection of problems expect to solve a collection of problems?

•

Can one habit replace another so that one can be habit-free?

TIME

TIME IS THE VERY CORE of this phenomenal existence. Without this function of duration, ordinary consciousness could not be.

Just as ordinary mind is truly a manifestation in Mind, time is a manifestation of the 'Timeless.' Time is the durational aspect of the Timeless that produces the phenomenal world of ordinary mind.

The now is Now but never now. For now cannot be now. By the time all sensory reports are sent to the brain and the images evoked, that portion of the event has passed. Ordinary mind is a record of the past, and it is never here now. The future is now but not yet known.

What we truly are is intemporal. The Now is the true observer, the 'I' which has no thingly or objective existence. The 'dreamed observer' lives in the land of never-now and yet is always in the eternal Now.

When there is a knowing of Mind, the durational aspect no longer predominates and we arrive in our natural abode—the Timeless. Yet, we should know that the Timeless and time are only two aspects of the indivisible. When the Timeless and time negate each other, then the Truth is.

This can only be known and not explained. All explanations require concepts and are durational in nature; they evade the negation that provides the indivisible Truth.

Yet, why are we so concerned with time? Many of us spend a lot of time looking for philosophies or religions that in some way give us more time. We seek immortality through our belief in reincarnation or in the belief that our existence will continue in a heaven (or even a hell).

But, for whom is it that we seek this immortality? Is it for this physical entity? Is it for this collection of vices and virtues? When we think of immortality, is it the notion that in some way this earthly personality will endure endlessly? Some will say, "No, it is not the body or personality that survives. It is the soul." But this is also an individualization which will cease when true unity is.

All images and theories are products of a bifurcating mind which depends on duration and constant change in order to manifest its presence. How then can ordinary mind (time) answer a question on eternity?

Zen reaches for a knowing in the Now. The practices are designed to help us disengage ourselves from the illusions of ordinary mind.

Satori, or enlightenment, provides a knowing of Reality. In Reality (the Timeless), there is no concern with immortality. For Reality is infinite and eternal; it is not dependent on a sequence of events.

If I aspire to live forever, I am then denying eternity. Instead of constantly reaching for the next moment, we should know the present, the Now. Then all the illusory aspirations to find immortality will give way to a knowing of the Timeless.

94

·

We should become aware that there is no objective past, present, or future for us. There is only an ongoing consciousness of change constantly occurring in mind. So it is that through time is produced only that which time produces.

If the complications of the discriminating consciousness are cut off and the truth of the Self Nature is present, there is no longer the appearance of someone restricted by time. The Now is now. Like an acorn, it is the infinite past and the infinite future all present in the infinite Now.

•

Just as an object cannot appear without a subject, time cannot appear without space.

•

It has been said that we are the dimension that provides consciousness—we are time.

Unk is objectifying time as if it was something outside of himself. But time is not a thing. Therefore, time is looking for time, or phenomenal mind is looking for phenomenal mind.

Yet, it is impossible for phenomenal mind to stand aside and watch itself pass by.

•

Neither do we!!

Even though the mind is full of memories and projections, it only has the Now.

102

•

Has your clock spoken to you?

·

The problem is not Foxy. It is Unk himself. Unk cannot overcome the problem because he projects it elsewhere. So the problem continues and Foxy prospers.

•

No matter how moving the revelations of the moment, Unk steadfastly holds onto his past convictions.

REALITY

MOST OF US SENSE that there is a power from which all things spring but from which we cannot see. We call it many names: God, Spirit, Absolute Reality, and so on. However, we live our lives according to our narrow perceptions of this phenomenal reality—the world of form. When we try to analyze our perceptions of Absolute Reality, it becomes apparent that the logical mind is incapable of knowing what it truly is. This is because the logical mind cannot ask a question without imparting its own ignorance and its clinging to illusion. 'I' feel that 'I' am a center of a world of multiplicity, and somehow 'I' maintain a distinction from that multiplicity.

When we ask questions concerning Absolute Reality, we forget that we are trapped by the illusion inherent in our relative viewpoint. The questions are faulty as they originate in mind which objectifies all things. How can we provide absolute answers to faulty questions by intellectual methods which are based on the same illusions that prompted the questioner?

Add to this illusion of separateness our deep conviction of the reality of time and space. Reality in ordinary mind is built on the foregoing. It is this conviction that provides our world-image with the illusion of a past-present-future unfoldment in time. We perhaps have never been aware of the fact that this past-present-future succession is just our way of interpreting our seeming reality.

Furthermore, there is no space in the world of the Real (no world either) except as it *appears* in ordinary mind. It is difficult for us to comprehend in a logical fashion that all these things that appear as spatially separated are not in the absolute sense separate. In this world of multiple images, even the Absolute is seen as a unity that appears as separate from our externalized world-image.

Thus, all of our questions on the subjects of Absolute Reality, time, and space cannot be answered because they originate in illusion in the consciousness of an illusory person.

However, just as the intellect is an instrument for use in the world of relativity, the bindings of the intellect can be transcended when an intuitive awakening to Reality occurs.

•

___

Apparently, Unk thinks he would know a real illusion from an unreal illusion. What would an unreal illusion be? Would it be Reality or an illusion of an illusion?

Does the knowing of Reality preclude the seeing of anything as unreal?

To know what an illusion is, is to know Reality. In a knowing of Reality, are not all things real? What then could be unreal? If it is real or unreal, it could not be absolute in nature. The Absolute is beyond the divisions of the dualistic mind.

Consider then, not real and not unreal—but the absence of the absence of both.

___

•

Master Woof's statement says it all.

•

Believing is not knowing.

Even the greatest of sages cannot impart their knowing to us. If we accept their words about knowing, we will only have a belief in their knowing.

The answer is knowing—and knowing that the knower is the knowing.

116

•

It is said that when phenomenal reality and the Absolute Reality negate each other, then the truth of Reality is present.

Very curious—who knows this? Since the Absolute is unknowable, how can there be a knowing of the negation?

If reality and Absolute Reality negate each other, what then is real? How can this negation be verified? The phenomenal reality is not fully cognized by ordinary mind, and the Absolute is beyond cognition.

How can Absolute Reality *be* if there persists the separation of reality and Absolute Reality?

118

•

Master Woof does not use the stick as a form of punishment. He is aware of the fact that Unk is always endeavoring to do the impossible. In other words, Unk wants the world to be other than it is. He wants to change it to suit his desires.

Unk always considers things as being either good or bad, or perhaps unworthy of attention. He cannot see the perfection in the natural unfoldment of life, nor can he see his inability to change the course of events.

Unk always seeks a means of escape. His search for the reality of life 'out there' is the crazy dance Foxy advocates to assist Unk in his effort to avoid life in order to find it.

When life can be lived as it unfolds, the foolish dance of avoidance is dropped, and life expresses life without the fantasy of an interfering self.

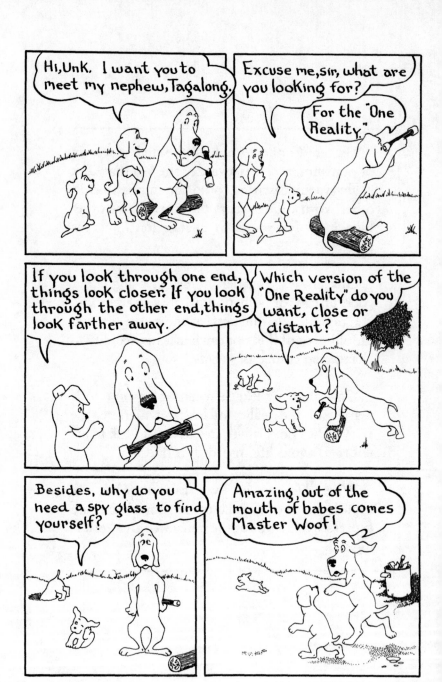

•

Unk's reality is that his Absolute Reality seems absent.

How does he know it is absent when it is unknowable?

•

Needless to say, Unk misses the point of Master Woof's words.

123

•

Whether Unk reads the words or tries to read between the lines, the Truth will still escape him.

If he clings to the words, he will be bound by words. If he clings to what's between the lines, he is still bound by his very activity of avoidance (of words), and by the 'deeper' concepts of Truth that he tries to read 'between the lines.'

•

The phenomenal world is a world of constant change. As such, there is no phenomenal activity or conditioning that can provide anything of an enduring nature.

If one seeks happiness or security in the world of change, only change will be found.

•

Does *not* knowing Reality make it any less real—any less what we are?

130

•

The seeming wants to describe the real.

What Unk needs is an eclipse.

•

True wisdom must reside in the heart as well
as the mind. Pepito's demonstration of friend-
ship brings out the truth in Unk.

134

•

Unk is not so concerned with discovering Reality. As usual, he is trying to find ways to avoid it.

•

Unk's egotistical attitude is shown in his pride in his running ability. He forgets he is laden with neurotic protective armor which protects ego but is an overwhelming obstacle in his so-called search for Truth.

138

•

The true 'I'—the real observer—is not known
because Unk still thinks of 'I' in a personal way.

•

Imitation brings the bitterest taste of all. If one pretense fails, another is put in its place.

142

•

The truth of this should be obvious.

ENLIGHTENMENT

THE MIND OF PHENOMENA, the mind of appearances, is the mind that wants to speak of enlightenment. The pseudo-self or 'thief' wants to speak of paths and goals. This is an egotistical effort to maintain itself, to perpetuate the appearance of a personality.

This ever-changing shadow, the pseudo-self, wishes to achieve and proclaim its enlightenment by claiming the sun as its own. It must be remembered that this little self cannot be enlightened since a full sensing of enlightenment removes the appearance of separation.

To point to something described as a goal and to name it 'enlightenment' simply creates profound obstacles to the Truth. If we look more carefully, we will discover that the phenomenal and the noumenal are inseparable. This being so, then all phenomena are enlightenment, and all beings are in this sense enlightened. In truth, enlightenment can claim ordinary mind as its own, but ordinary mind cannot claim enlightenment.

Unfortunately, there are many entities running about claiming enlightenment as if it were something that elevated them above other entities. Yet, whenever the pseudo-self maintains an attitude that it is enlightened, ignorance prevails. True, we are all enlightened—but in a non-separative sense.

There can only be enlightenment (satori) when the pseudo-self assumes its proper place, when phenomena and noumena function knowingly as one. Awakening is sudden, after which deliverance is gradual. Even after awakening, the accumulated karma (the old habit patterns) have a tendency to respond to circumstances in the old familiar ways. It is as if a pendulum has been disconnected yet continues to swing for a time before coming to rest. This slowing down is the gradual practice which is deliverance from these karmic habit influences. Thus, it is after satori that the way to true practice is open.

Enlightenment produces a balance between phenomenal understanding and the Universal Principle. The 'thief' is still present—yet only as an *appearance* in the whole.

146

•

The logical mind is at a dead end. Now perhaps intuition will be present.

147

148

•

Is blankness even possible?

·

Many of us believe that there must be an ultimate Truth (the moon). Often like Unk, we do not experience it directly—we simply howl at it.

•

Facing the Truth can be frightening for many of us. The seeming 'loss' of one's sense of personal self is the ultimate sacrifice.

For Unk, it is truly scary. He flees from the Truth and seeks a lesser truth that perhaps he can handle.

154

·

Up until now, Unk has gone around his practice rather than truly attending to it.

The Zen Master has had it with him. It is up to Unk from now on. He cannot return even for the comfort of the stick.

156

•

Foxy could be temporarily out of business. Certainly, he has lost his primary source of income.

Pepito now feels that Unk will somehow 'wake up.' If this turns out to be true, Foxy will be wise to file for bankruptcy.

·

The Old Goat in this sequence has a counter-part in real life. He represents an honored teacher well known to the author.

Many times in his long career, he has nudged students toward the Truth just as depicted here. He points out that Unk is (as we all are) the center of a universe that is infinite.

If Unk can stop thinking in terms of circum-ferences, he will find he is open to an unlimited Truth.

160

•

This is a page of clues. It is a direct pointing at something of vital interest to all seekers.

Unk has had satori. Now true practice can begin.

THIS BONE

IS

DELICIOUS

EPILOGUE

In the last chapter, Unk woke up. How did this come about? First, Unk gave up trying to begin at the finish. In his effort to find an 'Upside Down Circle,' he projected in his mind an idea of what it was. It was this projection that impeded his receptivity.

Finally Unk felt impelled to climb the mountain. Put in simpler terms, this meant to face the tasks of ordinary living. He succeeded in climbing the mountain. Unk then rested and fell asleep. When he awoke from this dreamland, he could clearly see the moon of enlightenment. This was not the reflection of the moon, as shown on the cover of the book, but the moon itself.

Now that Unk has had satori, he will function harmoniously with life's flow. Even though his old karma is still present, it is winding down, and Unk will no longer struggle to impose on the whole the whims of a fragment.

Zen Master (Ta Hui) Gilbert is a monk in the Cho Ke Order of Korea. He was born in Oakland, California, in 1909 and began the practice of Pranayama Yoga at the age of fourteen. After years of various yogic practices, he became involved in Zen and has since spent most of his life as a Zen Buddhist.

In 1973, Master Gilbert was recognized as a Zen Master by his teacher, the Venerable Dr. Seo Kyung-bo of Korea. Master Gilbert was given "Inka," the "Mind-to-Mind transmission," after which he was designated a Dharma successor in the United States to the Venerable Dr. Seo. He is often referred to as "Daishi" which means "Great Monk." This is a title for a Buddhist monk of high attainment.

Master Gilbert teaches and conducts services at various Zen temples in the United States. For over twelve years, he has conducted classes and intensive meditation retreats for English-speaking members of the Sambosa Buddhist Temple in Carmel, California.

The author is also a cartoonist whose work centers around Zen themes. Master Gilbert feels that humor is an effective way to activate an intuitive knowing of the truth of ourselves.

The Humor of Zen

Zen Master Donald Gilbert

Jellyfish Bones

The Humor of Zen

Zen Master Donald Gilbert

ISBN: 0-931892-21-X, 168 pages, 5.5 x 8.5, paper, $14.95

"Master Gilbert's book is a fresh approach to Zen. He does not adhere to tradition nor does he deny it. The work seems light and humorous, but his pen is a Zen sword and it is very sharp indeed.

"Humor is an integral part of Zen and here it is employed with consummate skill. Those who have studied under Master Gilbert know him for his gentle humanism. They know too that he can, in one flash of incisive wit, burst conceptual bubbles in a cascade of laughter.

"In the book be aware of the little dog with his bone. He is often depicted as saying, 'This bone is delicious.' This is a most important clue. This book, then, is a finger pointed at the moon. If the reader can stop staring at the finger and look at the moon, the moon will be revealed smiling back at the looker.

"When the little ego is recognized for what it is, then the Buddha will romp and play, filling the world with unimpeded laughter. Master Gilbert's book may just be the instrument that will help bring this about."

Ven. Dr. Seo Kyung Bo, Zen Master
of the Il Bung Son Won Sect in Korea,
Tripitaka (Scriptures) Master and
Master of Chan-pil Calligraphy

ORDERS: 1-800-643-0765 • WEB: www.bluedolphinpublishing.com

OTHER TITLES
FROM BLUE DOLPHIN PUBLISHING

Entering the Diamond Way
Tibetan Buddhism Meets the West
Lama Ole Nydahl
ISBN: 0-931892-03-1, 240 pp., 5.5 x 8.5, paper, $14.95

Riding the Tiger
Twenty Years on the Road:
The Risks and Joys of Bringing Tibetan Buddhism to the West
Lama Ole Nydahl
ISBN: 0-931892-67-8, 512 pp., 5.5 x 8.5, paper, $17.95

The Way Things Are
A Living Approach to Buddhism for Today's World
Lama Ole Nydahl
ISBN: 0-931892-38-4, 96 pp., 5.5 x 8.5, paper, $10.00

Rogues in Robes
An Inside Chronicle of a Recent Chinese-Tibetan Intrigue
in the Karma Kagyu Lineage of Diamond Way Buddhism
Tomek Lehnert
ISBN: 1-57733-026-9, 336 pp., 5.5 x 8.5, paper, $16.95

Cities of Lightning
The Iconography of Thunder-Beings in the Oriental Traditions
Samudranath
ISBN: 0-9660203-0-8, 216 pp., 8.5 x 11, paper, $24.95

ORDERS: 1-800-643-0765 • WEB: www.bluedolphinpublishing.com

CPSIA information can be obtained at www.ICGtesting.com
Printed in the USA
LVOW12s2138160114

369803LV00001B/56/A